What can I tell my Child about God?

by

ANDREA MARTINEAU

CONTENTS

D1808213

MOWBRAY
LONDON & OXFORD

INTRODUCTION

You have asked the question 'What can I tell my child about God?' Let's re-phrase that to 'What can I show my child about God?'

Your child is unique, and your family is unique, be it a one parent family or a commune.

We rarely try to explain the relationship between us to our children, we simply get on with living together.

A CHILD DISCOVERS GOD THROUGH THE ADULTS AROUND HIM

Now ask yourself a question
'What do I know about God?' You cannot answer the first question without asking that one. Be honest, because that matters most. The answer may range from, 'I don't know anything,' to the truly saintly, (although most of us entrusted with the care of children would fear to claim the latter state!)

Answering questions
The way you answer your child depends upon his age and personality, as will the way he asks his question. A baby cries because he wants an answer to 'Am I alone?' and he is picked up and cuddled. The teenager will put the question in a much more difficult and confusing way. While he still needs the same answer of loving, you also have words to share.

   Never be afraid to say 'I don't know'.

Who is this God?
Has it ever occurred to you that to your child God is rather like you. What does that say about him! Is God a God of love, joy, peace, patience, kindness, goodness, truthfulness, gentleness and self control? Don't worry. We need the ups and downs of family life to learn about reconciliation!

   A child discovers God through those who look after him. His picture of God is built upon his relationships with those who love him.

As an adult we need to look at our own childhood relationships with our parents and to see whether they help or hinder us in our approach to God.

A parent who is loving and accepting and non-judgemental towards a child shows the child that God is like that too. It's not what we say to our children about God, it's what we are.

But I didn't mean to say that

Tiny children have a habit of finding the most commonplace objects infinitely fascinating. They see a petal where we see weeds on a lawn. We answer our children's questions before they even begin to ask them. 'Put it down'. 'Leave it alone'. 'Come along, we haven't time'. 'Don't touch, it's dirty'. 'Hurry up for goodness sake'. 'For goodness sake STOP'.

Spend some time seeing through the eyes of your child. Become aware of the world. Who knows, you might see a dead snail as a thing of beauty too.

We don't have all the answers. To share the world in which we live, the family we belong to, is to discover more of God. We are already answering the question, 'Does God care, how do I know?'

The maker of patterns

As a parent you are a creator of patterns. Your child will copy and transform your creation. Enjoy life and do things together. Laugh and cry and discover and explore together. Tell your child by so doing that God is a God of life, of every minute of every day.

PRAYING TOGETHER

Wait a minute, I'll ask him
If we want to know something, we ask. If we want to
get to know someone, we talk together. We know
little of our friends unless we spend time in each
other's company. This same relationship with God is
called prayer. To find God we need to pray. To share
God with our children we need to pray together.

Starting out
Let's assume you're in at the beginning and your
baby is still in its carry-cot while you're looking for an
answer to this book's question. Now is the time to
start giving the answers to your child to pick up and
use in response to his questions.

   Many parents with a baby in their arms pray quite
naturally without putting thoughts into words. Do
you? But prayer also needs time, special time. A
good starting idea is for those sharing love with the
child to sit or kneel as the baby is put to bed, and to
be with God, deliberately.

Some prayers to put into words

> Thank you Lord for another day together.
> Thank you for your love for us while we sleep.

* * *

> Father, thank you for 'Peter'
> Keep us in your love now and always.

Thank you Lord for being a family.
Help us to enjoy each other and you.

* * *

Lord, sorry we were mad today,
Babies can be maddening.
Help us to have another go at loving tomorrow.
Keep us in your love.

* * *

Lord, I feel alone
But I love my baby.
Thank you for each other.

It doesn't matter if your child is playing. One day he will wonder what you're doing. It's a great gift to have a child ask a question.

Going a little further
Toddlers (and not only toddlers) love bed-time rituals. Life almost depends on them. His world is likely to go to pieces if familiar things don't happen when they should.

To share the beginnings of speech is a lovely time in family life. Now you have words to create patterns with too. Talk about the days' activities, and together say, 'Thank you Father God', for each moment remembered. Don't feel you all have to kneel down like Christopher Robin. Sitting by the fire, on the bed, in a chair, looking out of the window, and sometimes kneeling, are all good. When you tuck your child in and kiss him goodnight, perhaps use a final prayer which only you can create. May be 'Thank you Father God for cosy beds. Amen'.

Prayers are not just words

Remember that the time you spend blowing bubbles, watching water go down the drain, sploshing paint or flour together, these are prayers too. 'My parents gave me a sense of wonder,' is the greatest compliment you can ever have, and it is the paper on which to write many answers.

More early prayers

As your child grows and you talk together you will find that 'Love them Father God', follows quite naturally, as a caring for people met during the day or thought about. 'Sorry Father God', and 'Help them Father God', also fit in as your child's world expands. So prayer time becomes small thoughts of prayer with a response.

Sometimes it's good just to sit and look at something beautiful together – candles, leaves, shells, the wind, the rain, sun, fur, toys. You know what's beautiful in your world.

It's very easy to want a book of prayers when you're asking questions about prayer. 'Which is a good book of prayers?' you ask. It is not a question your child will ask. He responds lovingly to love, initially to your love, and then to God's love. It would be a strange love letter copied from someone else. Prayers prayed by other people, of which many are wonderful, belong to the older child, maybe as he approaches secondary education, when his world is becoming stretched in all directions. They will be all the richer for being set in the context of his own conversations with God.

The following pages are intended only as patterns.

Take what you see and create for yourself. Look at where you are. Look at God. And you will grow.

Night prayers

> God, you made the day.
> God, you made the night.
> God, you made me.
> Thank you for the light.

(Don't then go and switch off all the lights if your child is afraid of the dark. You don't learn to be happy in the dark because someone takes the light.)

> It was fun playing with Simon today.
> We had a lovely time.
> Thank you for my friends.
> And thank you for me.

*   *   *

> I did some good things today, God.
> It made me very happy.
> I expect it made you happy too.
> Thank you.

(Why are so many Christians so miserable? We should celebrate life.)

> I'm not very happy, God,
> Because I don't like Pam.
> She won't be very happy
> Because she doesn't like me.
> Please help us to be friends.

(God wants us to share the bad as well as the good.
It's O.K. not to feel good.)

Lord, soon I'll turn off my light
And soon I'll be asleep.
But soon others will have to go out in the dark
To keep your world alive.
While I sleep
Nurses care,
Cleaners clean,
Bakers bake,
Drivers drive heavy wagons,
Engineers make and use power.
Thank you for the hum of your busy world,
And thank you for my sleep.

* * *

Now, this minute,
Someone cries,
Someone laughs,
Someone lives,
Someone dies,
Someone is lonely,
Someone is loved;
I think about them;
I care.
Love them too Lord.

* * *

Father, let us sleep in peace tonight
So that tomorrow we can see what is beautiful.

Morning prayers

It's a new day, Hooray.
Thank you God for new things.

* * *

I've never lived today before,
It's all so new to me.
Yesterday was very good.
Help me Lord
To give a good day good things.

* * *

Lord I wish today was yesterday,
Then what I fear would be gone.
Help me to face today looking out
At all that is loving and good.

* * *

Today someone I don't know
Could become my friend.
I wonder who he will be.

* * *

I praise you God for water on my face,
For the wind that blows my hair,
For a hand to hold, for a face to smile,
For a world that's shiny and new.

Prayers for any time

Lord, I didn't see so many flowers
Until I looked.
Thank you for them.
Thank you for me.

When I listen
I hear.
When I look
I see.
When I stop
I grow.

* * *

Loving Father,
Bless
The people I walk with,
The people I walk past;
The people I talk to,
The people I listen to;
The people I laugh with,
The people I'm sad with;
The people I like,
The people I hate;
They matter to me.
I matter to them.

* * *

Lord, sometimes grass grows
In the cracks in the pavement.
Help me to be gentle
With growing things.

* * *

Lord,
The world is full of shoes.
They're all different.
They're all walking to different places.
Bring all the people who walk in them
Safely home.

When I feel happy,
Thank you for the sun.
When I feel sad,
Thank you for the rain.
When I feel loved,
Thank you for warmth.
When I feel lonely,
Thank you for cold.
Everything you make, Lord,
Needs sun, rain, warmth and sometimes cold
To grow.

* * *

Father God,
We all share the same world.
Help us to share
With each other.

* * *

Lord, I hope John's off school today.
I'm happier when he's not around.
Why?
Do you think he feels the same about me?
I wonder what you think?

(It's good to explore all our feelings, not just good
ones.)

Quick prayers for thinking

Come with me Lord.

Lord, you make me laugh.

I'm sad too, Lord.

Help me to find a way Lord.

This is good, thank you Lord.

Prayers when eating
For food,
For family,
For friends,
Thank you, Lord.

*   *   *

For the food you give,
For the love we share,
Thank you, Father.

*   *   *

God of the sun,
God of the rain,
God of the air,
God of the earth,
God of our food,
Our God,
Thank you.

*   *   *

For lovely things to eat,
For lovely things to share,
Praise to you, Lord God.

Lord of all,
You give, we share.
Thank you, loving Father.

* * *

For the seed you give,
For the people who care,
For the wonderful earth,
For those who prepare,
For those who go hungry,
With no-one to share,
We offer ourselves,
Loving Father.

FAMILY AND CHRISTIAN CELEBRATIONS

Let's celebrate
Christianity is concerned with celebration,
celebration of everything. Celebration of every
moment, whatever that moment is like.

The more we learn to celebrate the more we will
show our children of God.

We cannot provide answers to their questions –
their own experiences will do that. We can only
provide the bricks for them to build the house in
which to grow.

Each family is different. Each family needs to look
at the ordinary things it does and to make them
special.

The following are a few ideas, a few bricks with
which to begin building.

Birth days

Has your family grown out of parties? Are you no longer someone special? Are celebrations too much trouble? Let's hope not.

Each family has its own ritual of present giving. Perhaps the person whose birthday it is could give everyone else in the family a small gift. Let's celebrate together.

A birthday is a good time for looking at photographs and talking about 'when you were very small', or 'I remember when'.

Have a party, even if it's only a jelly. If adults don't celebrate, who will want to grow up?

At the end of the day talk about all the other birthdays, especially the original one. Thank God for all these things. We're all special.

Death days

The way we celebrate life will provide ways of accepting death.

Many children first encounter death through a pet. Through the caring for, and responsibility of, a pet, children are able to learn of the nature of love. The way we react with the child will provide many answers. The grief they experience is part of the same grief any adult feels at the loss of someone close. We need to feel free to express our grief, and the many other complex feelings associated with it, and to learn that we will survive if we are to learn to take hold of, and enjoy life.

Follow your child's lead. Some will want to talk more than others, but be sensitive to him, to his way. You set the stage for him to act out the drama. Reassure your child that it wasn't his fault.

Remember the good times. Be thankful there is no more pain. And above all, cry together. Death is a good time for growth.

Baptism days

Do you remember the celebrations of your child's baptism day. Why use this day only once. Make the anniversary of baptism a day to remember with a special meal, a trip, meeting with godparents, or tea with friends.

Many churches use a candle as part of the baptism service (Anglican Series 3) as a symbol of passing from darkness to light. If you still have one, use it in the week before the baptism day anniversary. Have prayers by candle-light, or a story, sit and talk, listen to music, or simply be still. Take the stub to church and arrange to be given a new one perhaps at the Communion. If you have never had a candle or have lost it, ask for a new one.

With a little planning and waiting, all the baptism days in one family can happen on the same Sunday in different years, then you can really celebrate.

A parish baptism on your special day is a real way of celebrating. 'Was I like that?' 'Did they do that to me?'

Christmas day

What are you going to tell your child about God at Christmas? Is it all tinsel and 'I want', agitated mums and opting out dads? Preparations have to be made, but the earlier the better. But preparations can help us to celebrate all the more, because we have joined in the waiting. Spend some time making presents. Giving takes time and loving takes effort.

The use of Advent candles, or Advent calendars (without fairies and Father Christmas please) help a child to gain a sense of timing. So many children are fed Christmas from October 1st, that they're glad when life returns to normal. Maybe putting up house decorations two weeks before Christmas, and the tree one week before, will provide sign-posts – and spread out the work.

If you are wanting to say to your child, 'God cares', then maybe inviting someone for at least part of your celebrations will show God in action. 'Is there any room?' is just as relevant today as two thousand years ago.

On Christmas Eve try a candlelight tea with lots of candles (night lights in foil baking cases). Invite some friends, sing carols, listen to the Christmas story and enjoy being together. In these days of freezers, preparations are not last minute affairs.

A candlelight breakfast on Christmas morning says a lot about the coming of light. Light a special new Christmas candle, light the baptism candles, light all the other candles, read the story of Christmas.

The symbolism of light is ancient – light, goodness, truth, illumination, the overcoming of darkness, 'I am the light of the world.' These things will become meaningful to your child. He will often be faced with choices about light and darkness. If his experience of light and love are strong, then he will have bricks to choose an answer.

Easter
Easter is about resurrection, about joy, about life, about the triumph of good over evil. 'What can I tell my child about that?' The use of symbols will help.

Use the same symbols as you used at Christmas.
Christmas and Easter belong together. Light can be
seen to be overcoming darkness as candles gradually
illuminate a room. Read the Easter story. Older
children can give each other the eggs they find – the
lesson is obvious. Celebrate Easter breakfast
together. Enjoy being in the light. Celebrate eternal
life.

Everyday
Everyday is special. Everyday we become more of
what we really are – if we dare. Everyday we
discover, experience, create and enjoy, and maybe
we suffer. Everyday we have lived for twenty-four
hours longer. Everyday we show our child more
about God.

If your family cares, God is seen to care. If your
family loves, God is seen to love. If your family has
time, God is seen to have time. If your family enjoy
each other, forgive and accept each other, then God
is like that too. Make time, eat together sometimes,
ask about each other's activities. Enjoy each other's
good points, accept each other's bad. Even stopping
for sixty seconds to have grace at a meal, or reading
a story at tea-time can change the day.

Use family activities in a positive way. Many
mothers work outside the home, and the dishes and
floors still have to be cleaned. We are responsible for
each other. These are our floors, our dishes. This is
our family. We offer help even when we don't want
to. Surely this is better than one person feeling 'used'
and on their own.

We're trying to say that God's world is like our
home. The same expressions of love and tension

arise. Use everything. A smacked behind is a
valuable lesson to learn about the love of God, but it
will only be valuable if forgiveness and
reconciliation, acceptance and love are all part of it.

COPING WITH THE CHURCH

What's a church?
A church building that isn't lived and worshipped in
is like a house before it becomes a home. Homes say
a lot about the people who live in them.

Young children love to explore, to look, to feel, to
investigate everything. Their world is still new, fresh
and exciting. Rediscover your local church, perhaps
your child will teach you new things.

Do you remember the last time you visited the
beach together? How you turned over stones, looked
at the cliffs, marvelled at the sea, splashed in the
waves, played games in the sand, breathed in the air
and tasted the salt on your lips as you listened to the
sea sounds. You used all your senses to discover and
enjoy.

Do the same to the church building. Choose a time
when there's no service, perhaps on a rainy day. Let
your 'under five' lead you on a journey. Even in your
own church you might find something new. Hide and
seek is a good game; ask the vicar to join in unless
he's too old to enjoy himself. God doesn't have
delicate ears – you don't have to keep saying 'ssssh'.
Touch, explore, look, discover and, just before your
child's had enough, take him home. Do this often.
The way your child feels about God's house matters.

What's The Church?

A house becomes a home when people live and love in it. A church becomes The Church when people live, love and worship in it.Your family has a vital part to play. Children above all, have the ability to make worship come alive. Some churches accept children as equals with adults, they acknowledge that we learn together and from each other. Alas, many churches separate their children to teach them their version of childish things. They're kept away from the holy adult who must not be disturbed at any price. If your church is like this you have a problem.

Coping with the problem

You can do one of three things. Firstly, opt out. Secondly, look for a church with more love. Thirdly, try to change the situation. The first is no solution – we need people to grow with. Choose the second or third depending upon your personality and courage.

Taking the plunge

If you're new to the worshipping community try to meet the vicar or minister and explain what you're setting out to do. Having explored the building you're now trying to explore the Church.

Many churches have family services. Some churches are enlightened enough to have a family Eucharist. Eating together is a basic experience for all of us. Choose a service where something is happening. Where there is music and movement and life.

Arm yourself with slippers, toys, crayons, paper, anything which is reasonably quiet. Slip in quietly during the more noisy parts of the service. Stay a while, then slip out again. The worship of God is continuous. It goes on all the time even when we are not taking an active part in it. We do not have to join in the whole service to make it valid.

Everything changes
People who are already members of the Church and then become parents face many difficulties. They have either to be overcome and used or they will overcome you. You may feel it impossible to worship with a baby or noisy child. You can't concentrate on the service. Red Riding Hood and the Holy Spirit don't seem to mix very well. The Peace of the Lord seems to belong to childless couples. Worshipping with children can be one of the greatest liberating influences in a life of faith. We begin to look at the Church rather than at ourselves. We belong to other people and they matter to us. The Church is worshipping together. Our love and concern for our children in church is as acceptable to God as the words of the prayers.

Quietness and stillness for yourself to be available to God belong to another time, but, if you do have that time, then quietness and stillness will still be there somewhere between the Holy Spirit and Red Riding Hood.

These are our children
The children of the worshipping community belong to all of us. We are responsible for them together. They will be there as we worship and will ask 'Why, Why, Why?' The way we accept them and smile at

them will provide part of the answer. What we do to our children, we do to Christ.

Don't give up
It's very easy to leave your child at a Sunday School or creche while you do your thing. But don't you want it to be his thing too? If we don't accept our children now, we can hardly wonder where they all are at eleven and upwards.

Children allowed to wander around the church during a service usually 'catch' the moments of quietness and become quiet. Other adults' pockets and bags are full of interest. It is doubtful whether many Christians are as interested in what is going on around them, or in one another, as our children are.

Some parents have decided to share their Communion bread with their children as a sign of their continuing nurture. We give our children everything else for their growth; why do we stop here?

God is not an abstract thought, a lovely answer, a solver of all problems, an insurance policy for good living, a preventer of hurt, a maker of nice people or an answer in words. God is a great disturbance. God is in us.

How much of God do our children experience in our relationships in the worshipping community and with them?

QUESTIONS AND IDEAS FOR ANSWERS

Why? Why? Why?
Children are always asking questions, usually the

most difficult and most important ones. They have an uncanny habit of catching most adults unawares. Any time is question time. Some children ask more questions than others. Even the parent who has sense enough to wait until asked to impart his ideas is sometimes frustrated because the question is never put. Atmosphere plays an important part in enabling children to ask questions. Where sex is a dirty word children are not likely to enquire about birth or life. The same applies to God.

Adults often don't ask questions. To ask a question implies that we don't know. We don't like to feel unsure. If we as adults are seen to be learning and discovering and asking questions, to admit to be wanting help, then we are giving our children something of great value.

Not because I say so
Some adults assume that children are incapable of thinking things out for themselves. They want to provide black and white answers which reflect their own views.

No adult has any right to provide a child with an answer without giving a reason, and without acknowledging that this is their own individual response. 'Why must I clean my teeth?' 'Because I say so,' is the obedience expected of a dog. 'Because I believe it prevents tooth decay and I am helping you to be responsible for your teeth,' is an answer which respects your child as a person. But, you argue, I can't always give a reason. Occasionally this may be so. The child who is respected as a person is more likely to accept your unqualified answer if ever the situation arises.

Here's an answer
We're giving answers all the time. Listen to some of the comments people make while watching television. They're quite revealing about what they really believe. 'Isn't that dreadful? They ought not to put it on.' 'Look at that, it's terrific.' Even the ON/OFF switch gives an answer. 'On' with 'Joberty Joke', 'off' with 'Report on Hunger' says more than words about priorities.

Our children ask many of the questions we daren't ask ourselves. Some of the answers are still being written. God is still revealing himself, still providing the answers. Sometimes, daring to ask a question exposes us to the possibility of having to accept an answer we don't like. Hopefully, we are always growing. When did you last change your opinion about something? It's a good sign. The only things which don't change are dead things.

Where to begin
Begin by being honest. Begin by living in your child's world. Start where his is with his own familiar things. To appreciate the ocean you must first feel water on your hand.

There are no set rules to answering questions. Each one of us is unique. You know your child and that knowledge and love is your guide.

However, as an offering to a more practical kind of help, here are some suggestions to help you feel your way to an answer. If you can't cope enlist help from someone you trust. If you cannot help provide the answers, ask the questions.

Some questions

Who made God? Basically you are wanting to say 'He has always been there.' But don't try! Eternity and God are not limited by our world of time. Between our birth and death we span out our time in minutes and hours. But outside those dates, what then?

So, begin where your child is. Talk together about the good and the boring things – favourite lessons, wet playtimes, about being ill, and about being on holiday. Time does not move at a steady pace. Time flies, time drags. Use the things around you. Look at a rubber ball, where does the surface begin and end? How about the stars? Can we really imagine vast distances or great numbers?

What we're trying to do is to present the idea that man has created time in its measured sense. We can't understand eternity. Say so. It's all right not to know or to understand.

Practically discover together more about man's measurement of time and distance.

Where is God? Help answer this one by refusing to sing all those 'above the bright blue sky' type hymns. The only thing man ever learnt about heaven from looking at the sky, was a sense of wonder.

God obviously is not in space. Today's child accepts that. On the other side of the moon is more moon.

We want to say that God is everywhere. God is God, around us and in us. Where good is, God is. God is not somewhere where we need to go to look for him. God is in the looking.

Beginning where we are again, talk about how your child knows you love him, how you know people love you. You can love even when you can't

25

see each other. You're part of each other. Certain signs tell us that people care, from clean socks to holding close. We know love by signs and symbols but it is not just in those things. Love does not need to live in one place, it simply is. God is, too.

How fat is God? This, and all similar questions should not be greeted with 'Don't be silly. God isn't like that'. The question was seriously put. Answering it, like many children's questions will set you asking more questions of yourself.

Well, what is God like? What's the answer. A parallel situation might help. Tom Smith has never seen his uncle in Timbuctoo but, as the years of letter writing and present giving pass, he has a picture in his mind about him. He learns more from other people who know him. He comes to believe in him as a wonderful person. No man has seen God, the Bible tells us. This question takes a lifetime to answer, because it's in the person of Jesus that we are given an answer to our questions about God.

We need to pray, to study, to talk with others, to read the Bible (a modern version – The Good News Bible is good for families) to give time to knowing Christ. The more we know, the more we discover there is to know.

But, back to the starting point. Get out some photographs of the family, especially those of adults as babies. Through your talking try to lead up to the idea that people look quite different at different ages although they are still the same person. A person is obviously more than just his body. 'We are the body of Christ,' is a phrase used in the Church's worship. God is God, and God is in us too.

Why can't I see God? Think together of all the

things you can't see but which, nevertheless, exist –
your breath, cold, warmth, smells, happiness,
sadness, the wind and so on. We can see and
appreciate what happens when they are present. We
know they're there just as the wind rustles the leaves.
Think together about the signs of God's presence.

Does God love bad people? We all grow up
wanting to belong to the 'in' group. It makes us feel
secure. There's all the more love for us if someone
else doesn't have a share. It takes many years to
learn that love isn't like that. Love loves regardless.
Human love sometimes gives up and dies because it
has its limitations.

Respond to this question by asking one. 'Do I still
love you when you're bad?' One of the greatest gifts
we can give to our children to build upon is the
foundation that they are loved as they are, good, bad,
nice or nasty. This freedom to be ourself creates a
whole adult who doesn't have to pretend to be
someone else because he feels inadequate and
unacceptable. Share what you as a parent feel like
when the child is bad. Is God able to be sad too? And
how about anger? Of course we feel angry with each
other. Anger brought out into the open teaches us
about our lack of communication and understanding.
Ignored, it is the death of loving.

Is God watching me? The Victorians frequently had
'potties' with eyes painted on the inside bottom
saying, 'Thou God seest all.' Some misguided adults
believe God is head of the secret police. 'What a
nasty nosey person he must be; I'll keep well clear of
him,' thinks the child.

Exchange thoughts with your child about the
loving watching that goes on between people,

between a mother and a child playing, between a child and a pet on a walk. What about the watching when someone's ill, or when someone's unwrapping a gift. God's got smiley eyes is a small child's thought. Maybe that's what we're trying to say.

Why did God let him die? This is one question which sooner or later we're all faced with. Ultimately it's not what we say but the way we respond which will be the answer.

Whether the 'him' is a pet mouse or a daddy, don't start uttering platitudes. Often this is one question which doesn't really expect an answer, for no answer will be able to dry the tears. Accept the tears, the hate, anger, guilt and the multitude of other feelings and share in them.

Don't say 'God wanted him', for that implies a God who doesn't care about all our loving or the way we feel.

This is not one of those questions which you can sit and discuss. It's too late. If your living has looked at life together, then that will, in its own time, provide an answer to death.

Be sad together. Grieve together. See through your child's eyes. You may see aspects of death of which you were not aware. Take time. Some answers take a lot of living.

Don't be afraid to say 'I don't know.'

Do animals go to Heaven? Don't feel you have to answer yes, but don't feel you need to say no and hurt the child. Talk about the ideas of heaven you both have. One father's idea of heaven is a place where everything that was lost is found. (From rompers to souls perhaps!) A God who cares about sparrows must care about animals.

Did God make everything? This is a great question really to enjoy. Use the library, films and TV etc. to find out about evolution. It's fascinating. You will discover more of God if you look. Talk to scientists who are Christians if you can.

God did not simply make things and leave them alone. He is continually creating. Use the family parallel of the care and nurture of children all through their life, continually helping them to become mature human beings.

What's The Holy Spirit? Children often hear 'Father, Son and Holy Spirit.' The latter, especially if referred to as the Holy Ghost, conjures up spooky beings. If the Holy Spirit means nothing to you, then you're probably reading this as someone as yet unconvinced by answers to your own searchings. We often begin our discovery of God by thinking about his Fatherhood. God the Creator. We learn of the things and nature of God through Jesus. Maybe we should begin our relationship with God by becoming aware of the Holy Spirit in us.

Talk with your child about all the things you're both good at, about all the things you'd like to be better at. Do you discover more as you grow? How about art? There is a story to share about a young child who wanted to become a great artist and watched a great artist paint. One day the child was given some brushes belonging to the artist. He assumed that now he too would be able to paint beautifully. He was discovered in tears. 'You would need more than the artist's brushes' said his aunt gently. 'You would need to possess his spirit.'

God is in us. Life is an opportunity to discover God's spirit in us.

CONCLUSION

So we reach the end of this booklet. You picked it up because you wanted an answer to, 'What can I tell my child about God?'. And you will be asking the same question tomorrow and for the rest of your life. God is not in the simple answer, all tidily folded and neatly packed, to a simple question. God is in the loving and caring, the happiness and sadness, the forgiving and acceptance, the living and dying, the discovery and growth, in the every moment in your parent/child relationship. You would never consider asking, 'What can I tell my child about good food?' You would take it and eat it together.

Our answers must do only one thing. They must set our children free to be themselves and to discover the God of questions. Together we may enjoy giving the answers.

SUGGESTIONS FOR FURTHER READING

Understanding Their World, by Margaret
Kitson.   (Lutterworth)
An absolutely essential book for anyone concerned
with the care and nurture of young children. It offers
practical help in building up those situations of
loving, providing and caring from which the concept
of God is gradually built. The first book to read after
putting down this booklet.

Focus on Meaning, by Joan Tough.   (Allen and
Unwin)
A book about language and communication, how to
listen to what our children are saying. Although a
book for teachers, it is written in simple language
and includes many examples of conversations.

Listen to the Children, compiled by Annejet
Campbell.   (Grosvenor Books)
Mothers from many countries talking about their
families. A good book to read if you need persuading
that love can grow from the usual family chaos.

Good Times with God, by Leonard Barnett.   (Hodder
& Stoughton)
A useful book for Christian families with children
aged 8 and above, who would like to spend a little
time sitting thinking and praying together in a
non-stuffy way.

Where do we go from here? by Rosemary
Haughton.   (Geoffrey Chapman)

Rosemary Haughton's own teenage children and a
group of their friends discuss religion, prayer,
churchgoing, sex, love, jobs, friends, and so on. The
results are unexpected. The author interprets them
against what family and school religious training has
tried to do, and asks 'Where do we go from here?'

© A. R. Mowbray & Co. Ltd 1981
ISBN 0 264 66747 6
First published 1981 by A. R. Mowbray & Co. Ltd
Saint Thomas House, Becket Street, Oxford OX11SJ
Printed in Great Britain by David Green Printers Ltd
Reprinted 1983